MRS. JOYCE A. BENSON

The One Left

❖

First Edition Book Cover Design, Editing, & Layout by:
Vincenzo Scipioni
@UnSeeingEyes

ISBN-13: 9780615840680
(Wood Press Publications)
ISBN-10: 061584068X

published by:

Wood Press Publications
P.O. Box 700
Saint James, New York 11780

To Mel

Contents

A Hard Reality: The Passing

❖

The ride home from the cancer center was sobering.

Cancer had spread even to the brain, so he couldn't chance driving.

The dreaded scourge had robbed him even of the legal right of final decision.

"Don't put me back in the hospital."

Fateful words conjuring up my worst of fears.

Called the Brain then back in high school, I had briefly toyed with the notion of being a doctor expunged quickly by my paralysis in the face of blood guts and gore.

Teaching was more antiseptic.

Death and Dying now sat next to me on the soft gray leather seat of my Denali. All of my scurrying and scouring, arranging and ordering could not forestall their arrival to my home.

Now, in this moment of the greatest gift I could give him loomed those darkling harbingers.

Today, that big brain of mine was of no use.

Today, IQ was irrelevant.

❖

*A*fter a 22 month valiant battle with large B cell lymphoma Mel finally died peacefully in our bedroom graced by the Hospice aide, that elegant shiny black man from Ghana on his left and me on his right side. "Help me prepare the body," were his soft yet commanding words. I needed to obey. We gently bathed him and dressed him for his final journey. I am glad I was there, present, not at the other end of a phone hearing the report from the doctor that he had passed. So, for me, because I had been and was in attendance to this final act, I could know that, yes, he was really dead. All of it was poignantly real.

I came down the stairs and made my way into the kitchen. My children were here somewhere in the house; I can't remember exactly where. I stood next to my friend Marianne who had brought bagels and was artfully arranging them in my large white rectangular serving basket.

We stayed in the kitchen mercifully tucked out of the visual path to the staircase and the front door. Thank God for the bagel ritual; I could concentrate on bread and vegetable cream cheese and ignore the two black suits who were carrying the corpse zipped into a body bag down two flights of steps and out the front door. I knew this was happening, but I didn't have to see it. Visuals are powerful. Images can linger.

The next few days were a mixture of quiet and hectic. My family was here: my son and his wife, my daughter, my siblings and their spouses, Mel's brother Bob, my niece. I know friends came and went, but I really can't recall much of this time.

I had never been very religious, was spiritual but not observant. Since Mel had refused right until the end to reveal what his final wishes were, it fell to me to do first what I was comfortable doing and second what would honor Mel's connection to his Jewish heritage.

With the help of Marianne I located a Rabbi who would speak at the memorial service the Sunday after Mel's death. I do not belong to a synagogue, so I had to search for a Rabbi. I had interviewed two other Rabbis on the phone (whom I rejected) as it was and is significant to me to have both Jewish and Christian family and friends recognized equally in the eulogy. Not only did I want a delivery of the traditional Jewish prayers in Hebrew, I wanted an open and loving address in English so all in the room would feel connected, significant and comfortable. My search was rewarded with an eloquent and perfect tribute to my dead husband and to his life.

Ironically, he had died just one day before his 70th birthday and his service was on my 65th birthday. Wow.

The Initial Cleansing

❖

I remember the day he died. I ran around like a lunatic stuffing construction-sized black plastic bags with all of the paraphernalia of sickness and death.

❖

First, I razed the bedroom: it took me only minutes to bag all the pillows, sheets, blankets, towels, even the comforter and drag the overstuffed sacks to the street just in time to meet the garbage truck. Next, went opened and unopened boxes of surgical gloves, pads, pills, thermometers, blood pressure monitor, all plunged willy-nilly into the bags and ferreted out to the street.

That morning I called Hospice and asked them to come immediately to pick up the hospital bed, the respirator, the oxygen. When I called, they told me they'd pick the stuff up in four or five days. My response was outrageous!

❖

"I plan to throw the shit out the window and over the second floor balcony if you don't

come today!" I guess I sounded irrational enough: the truck arrived later that afternoon and removed all of the death room equipment.

❖

The health aids that I actually owned also went out on the street: a brand new walker and a shower chair. Perhaps, I should have waited and donated these items, but I desperately needed to immediately cleanse the house of all of the end pieces of this two-year trial of death and despair. My advice? Get rid of as much of the end of life stuff as quickly as you can.

My long time friend Marilyn had driven up from Florida; her support proved to be timely and invaluable. My son Jon and his wife Heather had flown in from Wisconsin and were gong to drive back in Mel's Pathfinder.

Jon wore the same size clothing as his dad as they had similar body structures. It was Marilyn's idea to go through Mel's clothes so Jon could pack it into the Pathfinder for the drive home. She orchestrated the whole event as I sat on the edge of the bed in a semi-trance. In less than an hour, she had bagged clothes, some directed to Jon, some for the garbage, and the rest for the Viet Nam Vets, and that huge bag went on the front porch waiting to be picked up. All of Mel's dresser drawers and his entire closet were now totally empty. Mercifully, I would not have to dispose of his clothing. I was spared this incredibly painful chore.

If friends volunteer to help you in this very difficult task of clearing out your spouse's wardrobe, take the offer. Emptying closets and drawers by yourself would clearly be a huge trial. You may not do this clean out as soon after the death as I did, but time was short and both Marilyn and my son were soon leaving to go home.

A warning: don't hold onto the clothes; the longer you wait, the harder this will become. You run the risk of creating a "shrine" to your loss. You must put these intimate parts of your spouse to rest so that you can move on.

The Aftermath

You cannot withdraw from life, from the world, and curl up in a dark corner to grieve. Retreating into a coma state, retreating from yourself is the worst thing you can do.

❖

You are alive. Therefore, although you ache, although you fear, although you dismay, you must force yourself to push through the outward pieces of your life. If you do not, the inward pieces will never heal.

❖

What did I do that helped me function? I was proactive in creating and living through a schedule. Every little step counts, counts a lot. I awoke and immediately aired out my bedroom and then made the bed. Next, I showered and dressed, then drank the first of three mugs full of black coffee as I mindlessly penciled in the daily crossword puzzle as I was wont to do each morning clad in my pajamas. I would "order" my kitchen, bathroom, bedroom and clean for at least an hour. Tidying and cleansing my environment has always and still has the effect of tidying and cleansing my psyche! I then showered, did my hair and applied lipstick to feel normal, human and alive.

Get up, get dressed, get moving. Wear attractive clothing—feel attractive. Follow a life regimen day-by-day and hour-by-hour, so that you keep your life rhythm and your focus.

For me, staying with a schedule was key as I have no family here, no children nor grandchildren to spend time with, to rely on. Plan breakfast or lunch with a friend. Go to the beach; get out of the house and interact with other people. All the things that got me out of my house, out of my head and connected me to the normal rhythm of life were vital to my mental health and my emotional survival.

Each Monday morning as I have for years I drove 45 minutes east to Riverhead to my chiropractor, and because Tanger Outlet Mall is just a few miles down the road from his office, I would always stop to browse and shop, a double boon—adjustment and shopping, therapy and therapy!

In the spring, summer and autumn, I swept my front porch, weeded the flower beds, trimmed the ivy. Working outside in the yard is so invigorating and therapeutic.

In the spring I planted my geranium pots and my potted herb garden (I grow a load of basil to make enough pesto for the year).

For over a year after Mel died I stopped going to the gym, and I had been a gym rat for years. Well, I am proud to say that in the winter of 2011, I joined a new gym, hired a personal trainer and took my workouts seriously. Now, I try to go to the gym three to four mornings per week; I also work on core exercises at home with the big exercise ball and the half ball. In the last year I have lost 25 pounds and have toned and firmed.

❖

Looking good makes you feel good. Feeling good makes you "feel" good.

❖

Something else I have learned: don't worry about a master plan for the rest of your life. Not at the beginning. Maybe not ever. Just live through the moments. Get yourself centered and moving and the direction your larger path will take will take form. Anyhow, haven't you just learned that master plans don't work? The best you can achieve ever is a positive direction toward clear short-term goals.

Selling the House

In the spring of 2010, four months after Mel died, I put my house on the market; my plan was to move to Arizona near where my daughter lives. This was not a new plan as I had wanted to go to this area to retire for several years. Mel just *couldn't* leave Long Island, so I tabled my dream. Unfortunately, or perhaps fortuitously, the house did not sell. This has been the worst real estate market in decades, and to boot, I have a very unusual house that does not appeal to the average buyer. Just before listing the house I trekked out to Scottsdale and spent a week with a realtor looking at houses in the north Scottsdale area. I scoped out all of the logistics to guide me in the incredible task of moving across country and starting over in a new place, alone. I came home and typed out spread sheets detailing my living costs, so I could weigh the economic and other pragmatic advantages of the move: no winter, one level house, desert landscaping.

All of my friends told me it was too soon, that I was making a huge mistake, that I was running away. Although there was probably *some* truth in their assessment, I think my decision was more complicated than that. As it was, the house didn't sell in 2010 or 2011, so I resigned myself to staying. I would have to postpone my plans of leaving my home, my friends, my comfort zone. This was another profound lesson: there are many outside forces in my life that I just can't *control*.

Had I gone so soon after Mel's death, I would not have had the support of friends, doctors and all the other fail-safe pieces of my personal network. Who knows? If the house had sold and I had gone west *then*, could I have moved through the process of grieving and healing? Speculations are just that, speculations.

So, today, where does the move stand? Winter has come and gone and I have just completed the spring cleanup and planting. Do I plan to move? Absolutely. My 68th birthday is now almost six months past and I know definitively that as the years pile up, the demands of maintaining this house and property will grow beyond me. Yes, the house is again up for sale.

❖

Whether I stay or go, I must make new friends, form new relationships and construct an entirely new life paradigm. Staying just "looks" more comfortable.

❖

Taking Care Of Business

❖

Yes, I knew death was coming, so I don't know how to speak to people who lose a spouse with no warning at all. I'll have to leave the managing of the shock and subsequent trauma of sudden death to the experts. But the logistical aftermath is the same. And whether you're ready or not, you have to take care of business

❖

Remember this: You will be in a fog for quite a while. So, you will need to write things down. Keep a pen and a large yellow pad on your kitchen counter where you can readily locate them each day. Keep a weekly or monthly calendar book adjacent to them. It is more than three years since Mel's passing, and I still keep these tools right there in my kitchen because I am alone and the responsibilities are totally mine.

Thank Heavens I have always been an OCD over the top record keeper. Where do you begin to take care of business? Start making lists: note garbage pick-up days, turn on or off the sprinkler system, empty the dehumidifier and/or fill the humidifier, schedule the car for an oil change, call the accountant to schedule an appointment for taxes.

Take out the checkbook or check on-line records. See which bills will be coming and when. Check your checking account balance. If you have a comfortable income and balance in your account, pay the bills as they come in immediately. I do this so I don't misplace bills and forget about them. I put the snail mail bills on the little table in the front foyer and mail them immediately. Be very careful to guard your credit rating.

❖

Before you begin the daunting task of af-ter-death business, you must first gather all the documentation that you will need and insert papers and cards into the appropriate of three folders labeled: Immediate Action, Pending, and Completed Business. This way you have an easy and automatic in-your-face, on-your-kitchen-counter organizational

and record keeping system until the process,
which could take months, is completed!

✤

Gather up your spouse's credit cards, his Social Security card, his Medicare card, the original copy of his will, copies of all investment data—IRA's 401K's and all other investment accounts, both joint and separate, and life insurance policies. Store these items in the appropriate folder for immediate action.

✤

Cancel his credit cards immediately.
Purchase Death Certificates.
Call Social Security to report the death.
Call Medicare and all other service providers.

Call life insurance companies to start the pay-
ment process.
Schedule appointments with your attorney,
your financial advisor and your accountant.

❖

Don't ignore or minimize any of these steps. Your spouse's death does not excuse you from major legal and fiscal responsibility and liability. Keep a record (your yellow pad) of every phone call you make. Ask the representative you speak to for his/her name and title, note the time, the date and the substance of the communication.

When I cancelled Mel's credit cards, I requested an email and a snail mail written confirmation that said cards as of that date had a balance of zero. Demand names and positions of anyone you talk to. Demand hard copy snail mail verification in addition to email communications. And save these documents. As you receive responses, move the paperwork from the *Immediate Action* folder to either the *Pending* folder or the *Completed Business* folder and store these records in an easily accessible, secure place. Then, shred the credit cards! Shred all old bills from these credit card companies; you don't want those card numbers to go into your garbage, then into other hands.

Hopefully, when you made funeral arrangements you requested (you have to pay for them) at least ten "original" death certificates. Some of the "business" you will need to conduct will demand originals (they have a raised seal). Other business will accept copies, so ask which type of certificate is required. Keep these certificates in the *Immediate Action* folder on your kitchen counter.

Immediately contact Social Security. You must inform them of your spouse's death, so they can stop the monthly direct deposit payments. If you ignore this advice, you will have to repay any deposits made to the account. On another note, I missed out on the one-time Social Security payout of $250 because I just didn't know in time to file for the money and, consequently, missed the deadline.

Call Medicare and apprise them of your spouse's death. Call the local utility provider (electric), your oil or gas company, your cable company, your exterminator, your phone company or companies, water company and put all of these accounts into YOUR name. Go to your bank and or banks and bring a couple of original death certificates with you. You must change all accounts to your name only. If you have not established your own credit score over the years, you must start now! Hopefully, you already have a credit card in your name. If not, immediately apply for one. Try living in this world today with no credit card or credit score! It would be a daunting challenge!

Life Insurance payment can go smoothly, or it can be a nightmare. First, locate the policy or policies. Also, find paid receipts showing continuous payment since the initial activation of the policy. Know what kind of policy this is and exactly what it entitles you to.

❖

Do not expect the company representative to be your friend. He or she is not. Knowledge and records are your allies.

❖

One of Mel's life insurance policies (to the tune of $100,000) was initially denied payment because the processor didn't "notice" that the policy had been converted, not started, in the three years before his death. Thank goodness I had all the paperwork and cancelled checks proving the policy had been active up to the date of his death since 1987! Their response? Oh, we're so *sorry...* we'll send your check immediately.

❖

I wonder how many life insurance claims are not honored, and how many millions of dollars are not paid because beneficiaries don't have the necessary documentation or do not know how to navigate these murky waters.

❖

Call the life insurance company. Write down the instructions they give you. You will have to surrender the policy and submit an original death certificate. Keep written records of all communications.

Make an appointment with your attorney. Even though you are the sole beneficiary of the estate, the will must be read and processed. I had to have my house assessed and the value documented for the tax record. Know that you will have to either do or redo your will to designate new beneficiaries, new powers of attorney, new health care proxy. Things have changed. It's up to *you* to protect your future and your assets.

Schedule an appointment with your financial advisor. Mel's IRA was simply transferred into my account as I was his sole beneficiary. The rest of the investment portfolio had been in both names, so that putting everything in my name only was pedestrian.

Next, see your accountant. This job for me was not necessary until spring before tax deadline time as I had been the record keeper and the financial manager in the marriage. If your spouse had these responsibilities, then you must see your accountant immediately and learn what you need do to take the fiscal reins.

Persistence and tenacity in these painful but necessary duties will put your life in legal, logistical and financial order. Do not dismay and do not give up. Remember, it can take months to finalize all the business of death.

Reevaluate The Home Front

If you don't already have one, have an alarm system installed in your home. I have a dual system; the second is a battery-operated backup. Also, make sure the system has a fire alarm alert. Go to the hardware store and buy a carbon monoxide detector. Plug one in an outlet in your bedroom near the floor. If the detector is above the level of your bed, as you sleep, by the time the alarm goes off, you'll be dead. Put another low to the floor in the kitchen or somewhere on the first level.

If you live in a temperate or a cold climate, do business with a large reputable oil firm if you have oil heat. Be sure to schedule annual furnace cleanings and tune-ups. Going with a fly-by-night company to save money on fuel oil is not cost effective when you need a service person in the middle of the night when the temperature dips to the single digits. My contract includes service day or night and maintenance.

Have you're your gutters cleaned twice per year. I forgot to have that annual spring cleanout and then we caught the remnants of Tropical Storm Andrea which deposited 1-2 inches of water per hour on Long Island.

What happened is that the torrents of water spilled over the side of the clogged gutter and filled the three window wells below. I spent about 8 hours intermittently bailing and pumping the water out of these depressions so that my basement wouldn't flood. Did I mention that I was soaked to the skin in the driving rain each time? Had I remembered to take care of the gutter obligation, I would have saved myself a lot of work and stress and exhaustion!

Scrutinize the outside access to your front door. Have motion detector lights installed to light your way from your home to your car. Have large obscuring bushes or shrubs trimmed or removed from the front of your home. Be certain that your property is cleared of junk or debris to eliminate the chances for falls and accidents. Protect yourself in advance.

❖

Think of the unthinkable and eliminate the variables that would put you in harm's way.

❖

The Little and Not so Little Things

Mel and I had always gone to Costco together to stock up on everything from bottled water to laundry detergent to lawn fertilizer. It was a ritual. And part of that ritual was that he would carry the heavy items into the house. Now, clearly I go to my favorite warehouse superstore alone. I no longer buy many items in bulk. I also notice what items would be too heavy for me to lift and transport. Yes, even shopping requires a different mind-set.

Find a reliable and talented handyman. Even though I am very capable and even though I have done all kinds of yard work, painting etc., I gladly admit that heavy work is a bit beyond me now. I am in great shape for 68, but it is stupid for me to attempt to perform chores that are potentially dangerous. I can't lift very heavy items or bend for long periods of time or I put my back out. Fortunately, I can afford to hire people to do what I cannot do. When I sell my house, I will move into a more senior single friendly structure: one level. If you can't afford to maintain the house, you'll have a major decision to make. Face that financial reality and face it quickly. You may have to sell your home and move into a less costly apartment or condo.

Be certain that you have an updated and reliable smart phone. If you don't have one or don't know how to use one, get one and learn. You must become facile and comfortable with the cyber world. Keep your mobile phone with you whenever you leave home. Enter the numbers of all of your friends and family in your contacts. Keep a list of other key people including your pharmacy, your doctors, your accountant, your lawyer, your clergyman, AAA, your auto insurance agent and the accompanying addresses and phone numbers in your contacts. Having this contact information at your fingertips is essential now that you are alone.

If you are living alone and are truly alone—that is with no family near by—then you need to give serious pause to emergency protocols in the event that… In the chapter *You Can Do It*, you'll read that six years ago I had fortuitously insisted on buying and installing a generator and thank heavens I did, as I have now lived through the aftermath of two hurricanes and the subsequent power outages since Mel's death.

Another thought. Stay in touch with either a friend or family member daily. Someone needs to keep tabs on you in the event that you find yourself in an untenable situation—like falling, for example. Keep your cell phone charged and with you at all times even at home, or get one of those alert devices. As you get older, you may want to rethink your living options to reduce the possibilities for harm in your life. I'm doing that now. It's a sobering experience for someone like me who has always been *in charge*.

Face Your Little Demons and Pamper Your Car

For many years I accepted many ridiculous little fears as facts of my life that would never go away. *Wrong.* One of them was that I was very uncomfortable parking in a multilayered parking garage. Well, Mel had ten hospitalizations at a large university hospital replete with large parking edifice. And to make this charming discomfort more poignant is the fact that I drive a large Yukon Denali! Since I was going to the hospital twice a day off and on for almost two years, I was forced to not only face and expunge my fears, but also learn to navigate the rounds and curves of the garage with facile expertise. I even began to enjoy playing *chicken* with *horses' asses* who tried to steal a spot that I had patiently waited for. Since vehicle size and bulk do count, I am proud to announce I always won. Another of my silly but real fears was going down into the basement alone at night in the dark. And that limitation is also now gone—poof! The basement dark or light is just another level of space and storage to be visited at any all times.

While I'm on this pragmatic rant, let me emphasize the importance of your vehicle. Although I always have always taken my cars in for repairs and maintenance myself as Mel worked six days per week, he had always been there for backup. Tend to maintenance, oil changes, and inspections regularly. Keep your car in tip-top shape. Check that your tires have enough tread—be sure they are not losing air and have them rotated and balanced. If you have a flat tire or if you break down, you need to have an emergency service ready at your call. If you don't belong to AAA, join. I have been a member for decades and have found their service to be prompt and reliable both on the road and in my driveway. Remember, your automobile is your moving connection to the world, and you need to keep it in top operating condition!

Go to the dealer where you purchased your car and have a couple of extra keys made. Put one in your purse and keep another in the house. As zoning out is a reality of the grieving process, you need to create fail-safe guarantees that you won't be locked out of your car. While we're talking about keys, give a house key to a family member or to a trusted neighbor. Don't hide keys outside in the yard; burglars know this trick. Again, you need to keep creating layers of safety netting. Get busy. There is no spouse to call in an emergency.

Good grief, I can't believe that only a day after writing this entry that I lost the ignition key off my key chain outside our local bakery, and I just couldn't find it! Thank goodness I had a spare in the secret zipper compartment in my purse.

For Those Who Are Not Yet Alone: Preparing

❖

This chapter is directed to those spouses who have not yet lost an ailing partner or to those who are approaching an age where the demographic, ethnic, genetic and longevity statistics start becoming an ostensible and insidious reality.

❖

How many wives over the years have relinquished the "finances" to their husbands? Do you know what your monthly, yearly financial obligations are? Do you know how to navigate a checkbook or how to pay bills online? If the latter, do you know the account locations, numbers and the passwords to access each?

❖

When it's too late it's too late.

❖

Is your name on all bank and investment accounts? And then there's the *little* matter of health insurance—under whose name is the primary (if you are under age 65) or secondary policy carried? If it is your spouse, do you know what to do in the event your spouse dies? Educate yourself, now. Stay abreast of the provisions and limitations of your health care coverage.

Let me speak for a moment to you gents out there whose wives manage all of the "business" aspects of the household. *You* could be the spouse who is left! Listen to the above advice and take the following steps to get yourself informed and empowered.

See a lawyer and have a will drafted. Include health care proxy and durable power of attorney. Make sure both spouses know where the original will is stored. Apprise a trusted relative or friend of where you have kept these documents.

Establish legal guardianship for any under-aged children.

Make provisions for pets.

Photocopy fronts and backs of cred-it cards, Medicare cards, health insurance cards, Social Security cards.

Have a portfolio housing proof of your investments and name of and relevant data regarding your financial planner. List all an-tiques, jewelry and other valuables; describe them and ascribe a ballpark value and then note where these things are.

Have in a folder life insurance policies, mortgage agreements, deed and title to house, bank account statements, Medicare records, list and description of all doctors and medi-cations for both spouses, key to safe deposit box, income tax records, title to vehicles, tax documents and forms, and the list goes on.

Pay off all debt; live beneath your means and sock away savings; make investments. Keep at least five thousand dollars in a liquid savings account or in cash. You don't want to be stuck with no hands-on funds.

Be sure that each spouse has two credit cards separate from the other's. Alternate bill paying using all cards so each spouse establishes his/her own credit rating.

Finally and most painfully, *talk* to your spouse about your final resting plans. This was the step that we had omitted, and that omission caused indecision and much discomfort later. Mel had always been *more Jewish* than I, so I really didn't think he would be comfortable with *my way* of disposing of remains. Both before and after he was in Hospice care, I attempted to get his response: did he want a traditional Jewish funeral and burial? I would have honored his request. He simply would not answer me. In the final days of his life I asked the Hospice social worker to broach the topic one more time; he hurled pillows and any other projectile within his reach at her and threw her out of the room. He simply was not interested in death; life was what he desperately wanted.

❖

By default, he left the death stuff to me.

❖

So, almost a week before he died, I sat in my kitchen with the local funeral director making out a check to prepay the expenses of "direct cremation" and the rental of the large room in the beautiful new funeral parlor for the memorial service. Can you imagine having to do that? Gladly, I had enough foresight and fortitude to make these final arrangements a few days before the fact; later would have been unbearable. I'm certain that some relatives were unhappy with my decision. Remember, you owe the extended family nothing; this is not their decision. Honor only your spouse, yourself and your children.

❖

Perhaps the most valuable advice I can give healthy, active senior spouses is to first acknowledge your own mortality and the mortality of your partner. Death is not something that happens "just" to other people.

❖

Then, sit down and *talk* to your spouse, really *talk*. Gather all the relevant documentation and draft a plan, *together*. Another thought. If you have the means, pre-plan and prepay both of your "final arrangements" now, while you are centered and rational and healthy. This step will guarantee that your wishes are honored after your passing and will save the surviving partner much pain and indecision later.

I truly wish we had sold our home and had relocated to Arizona years ago as I had desired. Being a widow, a woman alone taking care of the demands of a large home is daunting, indeed. Had we downsized then, together, moved west then, together, my life *now* would be much less demanding. Assess your living arrangements and create hypothetical scenarios of how each of you would live if the other died. Project into the future and take an honest look at your home, your possessions, your property and your physical health and condition.

❖

Crunch the financial numbers together. Answer these questions. Could either spouse singly afford the fiscal obligations of supporting the home? Could either spouse singly handle the physical demands of caring for the home?

❖

Get rid of all superfluous accumulations, now. One of my friends who lost her husband a year before Mel died had done just that. She and her husband had sold their house and purchased a condo in a senior community. They took very little with them into their new home: they bought new furniture and home goods. So, when her husband passed, she was in a comfortable, manage-able and single-friendly environment.

❖

Is your home jammed with a thirty or more year hoard of stuff that the surviving spouse will be choked with later? Truly, I know that reality. Do your "final cleanout" now!

❖

Can't Sleep

2 2 months of acting as advocate and caretaker for Mel came with great cost to me. Never before had I had difficulty falling and or staying asleep. But during this time, he endured round after round of chemotherapy—had ten hospitalizations.

❖

The first thing that happened was that I couldn't sleep in the marriage bed.
Then, I just couldn't sleep.

❖

I now suspect that this insomnia came in part from being in a fight or flight mode most of that time. Not only did I manage the entire house, run my business, but I also had to wage war with the hospital so that bureaucratic stupidity would not cause Mel's death. I never stopped working, running doing, moving. It wasn't till much later that I realized the magnitude of this unending stress.

Mel had aged a hundred years in the first three month of the illness. I just couldn't look at him in bed. He looked like a corpse. Also, chemo causes the patient to have foul smelling gas (chemo farts as they are called). Our bedroom became his sickroom. So, I would sack out on the second floor couch in front of the television each night. Flipping through the channels for an eternity, I would finally fall asleep with the picture going and the audio on mute. A good night would be waking up only two or three times. The typical night meant waking every hour and a half, so for almost two years I was sleep deprived. I couldn't risk taking sleeping pills because of the deadly oak staircases in my house—one of the possible side effects of sleeping medications is sleep walking. I just couldn't risk it.

What I didn't know then was that this insomnia would continue and become the new *normal*. At first, I thought that changing my sleep environment would help purge the insomnia. I had chucked all the bedding and towels after Mel died, so I had to go shopping. Then, I cleaned the bedroom and the master bathroom with a vengeance. I took great care in making up the bed in the new sheets and comforter. I had to make it new. I had to make it mine. But, some nights the new trappings just didn't matter. So, I would just end up on the couch doing the channel surfing ritual until I dropped off to sleep.

Where does the insomnia stand now? All last fall and winter while I was in a dating relationship my sleep patterns began to normalize. But, since July, since the reawakening of loss and pain, sleeplessness has again become a nightly problem. I have tried many over-the-counter aids, to no avail. Presently, I'm looking into Tai Chi and meditation as non-medical means of quieting my mind so I can embrace sleep. It's just a work in progress.

Waves of Grief

❖

They just come over you. You can't control them.

❖

Sometimes they happen when you're sitting watching the television. But usually they're triggered. And after a long-term marriage living in the same house for decades, there are literally hundreds of "things" that are triggers to that wave.

❖

The pain of finality. The pain of loss. The pain of aloneness. It's paralyzing.

It's in your chest. Sometimes it's a tight angst that just won't stop, and sometimes it escalates into a full panic attack where you want to get up and just run away and at the same time you can't breathe.

❖

Mornings and daylight hours were manageable. In fact, they were almost normal. Something there is about the light that is cleansing and soothing. And also during the day I was always purposeful and goal-directed and moving.

So, what did I do? I went to see my doctor. I refused antidepressants but did accept a controlled low dosage use of Xanax. When one of those panic moments came upon me, I would do deep controlled yoga breathing calmly repeating silently to myself that this would pass. And it mostly did. If I couldn't pull out of the angst, I would take a Xanax, the smallest dosage .25 mg, sometimes half of that. And in a few minutes, the pain would pass. Remember, I was under a *physician's* care as I went through this process. Don't *borrow* meds from friends; get and follow professional medical guidance.

My dear friend Joel (who was also Mel's dearest and closest friend since childhood) lost his wife about 18 months after Mel died.

He chose to use both a grief counselor and attend a grief support group and these options were very meaningful for him. What I'm trying to say is there is no one "right" way to deal with the pain of loss. Work with your doctor, clergyman, family. Find what works for you.

❖

Unfortunately, a lot of the people in your life will give you "armchair" advice that is well-intentioned but patently useless because they just can't understand what you're going through. How the hell could they?

Empathy doesn't give you the capacity to really grasp this kind of emotional angst!

❖

Now, I am glad that during and after the grieving process I refused sleeping pills and I refused antidepressants. Hindsight has given me the comfort of saying I pushed through it, that I toughed it out.

But, it is time that has granted an understanding of myself in the whole after-death process. In the first stage after Mel's death, I *muscled* my way through the anxiety, the panic, the pain, the angst. What have I always done in my life to solve problems big and small? Stand tall, think, make a plan. Get up early, create a schedule. Work from dawn to dinner. Hey, they always called me the *Big Gun*. I put my house on the market four months after the death. I worked day and night to clear the inventory out of the house. I cleaned and ordered and readied the house to be shown. I kept busy; I was always productive.

All of this proactive effort was thera-peutic and restorative, but it was not enough.

❖

What I was to learn as time went on was that to exorcise pain, first you have to surrender to it. Embrace it. This doesn't mean you should wallow in a sloth of depression.

It means that you have to "feel" l it through to its end to deplete its power—or it will come back and bushwhack you as it did me.

❖

The Alone

❖

*After all of the hullabaloo and after all of the
cards and after all of the relatives went home,
I was actually glad to be alone. For a while.*

❖

I had never before been alone. I had
married just shy of my twenty-first birthday. I had graduated from college in

June of 1965, started my first teaching job in September of the self-same year and married on Thanksgiving Day. A busy year indeed!

In those ancient days "good" girls did not live with their boyfriends before they married. In fact, even though it was the mid-sixties, we all preserved the illusion that we weren't really "cohabitating" with our boyfriends and that marriage would, of course. sanctify the deal. So, I married. Was married for 44 years, some happy, some not. This is not going to be a tell-all of the ups and downs of a multi-decade marriage. Rather, I wish to make the point:

❖

I did not know "how" to be alone. No one had ever given me the tools. I was truly in an alien land.

❖

Maybe some people do adjust to and even prefer living alone. I don't think I will ever do the latter. And when I think I am adjusting to being a singleton, I get a brisk slap to remind me of how much I hate standing alone. I'm thinking of Dana's wedding two years ago. She is the daughter of a neighbor family with whom I have been close for more than 25 years. Jeannie, my friend and mother of the bride, seated me at a table of couples of other teachers. Remember, I said couples. I was the only single. Of course, Jeannie thought this placement would be perfect because I knew some of these folk, and we were all teachers. I wasn't prepared for the feeling of aloneness at that table when all the couples got up to dance. Not that I spent 44 years velcroed to Mel's side—it was just a symbolic zap. Guess what girl: you are alone! Not that I haven't attended all sorts of events alone in the past—good grief, I was a teacher and a business woman.

❖

But that night handing the valet my ticket alone and getting into my Denali alone in the pouring rain and going home alone trumpeted in and around my head alone, alone, alone... and it's dark and it's raining and you're going into a dark house, alone.

❖

So, the TV becomes your friend; it makes noise; it has people, action, and color as it pretends life. And right now pretend life, a virtual world, they're welcome because they are something and you need something!

❖

You sit with the remote. Spend hours flipping through the channels. Little engages your full attention. The evenings bring the darkness. In the light you fare much better.

❖

But the darkness envelops you in a whole other horror. It merges blips of panic with claustrophobia.

❖

In my case, I was alone most evenings because I have no relatives living near by. Both my son and my daughter live out of state—same for my siblings. Sadly, I have no grandchildren. Neighbors and friends are wonderfully supportive, but they have their families and they have their own lives and rightfully they should, and you can't and you shouldn't impose your aloneness upon other people.

Eating Alone

Breakfast and lunch are not problematic. Because both Mel and I had both worked full time, the two daytime meals, if we ate them, were always apart. But dinner was different. We always ate dinner as a family, and since I love to cook, most of the dinner meals were here in my kitchen at home. The table was always a presentation; food was plated and eye appealing; the table was always set. My family did not eat in front of the television. We ate together at the table and we talked; we interacted.

First, there was no motivation to cook at all. So, I prepared the simplest of meals just because I had to eat. Now, I cook sporadically. In the summer months I do a lot of grilling simply because it's easy and quick. Also, most meals that require much preparation produce too much food. It simply is not easy to cook for one person. So, one solution is to make a pot of Italian sauce and to freeze single meal containers. I have in my freezer now several chicken parmesan dinners ready to pop into the oven. Last winter I froze all kinds of meals, even roast brisket and mashed potatoes. All of this is quite doable.

❖

The hard part is eating alone. And eating dinner alone is deafening. Most times I either eat very perfunctorily in the kitchen or I drag a tray of food in front of the television. I still have not grown accustomed to the austere truth of sitting alone peering down at my plate of food.

The daily eating ritual is a daily reminder of the reality of the empty chair just to my left.

❖

Since I was a child I have loved to cook and to bake. Preparation of food for me was not just a life necessity; it was an expression, an act of love, of nurturing. When our family was young, we had a huge garden in our back yard; it was very prolific in its output as the property had been a potato farm and had inches of top soil enriched by the nutrients from our compost heap. Not only did I bake and freeze pies, I canned and preserved jams, pickles, peaches, applesauce, dark red cherries, bushels of tomatoes. I grew basil and froze the resulting pesto. I made everything from *scratch*—from soups to blueberry muffins.

My house hosted the holidays year after year, decade after decade. I cooked and prepared so very many meals and celebrations. Thanksgiving was always my favorite feast. The menu varied little; this was not my idea as the family and the other "regulars" demanded it. Fresh killed turkey from my local butcher filled with chestnut stuffing, homemade gravy, freshly made cranberry-orange sauce, homemade cinnamon applesauce, Yukon gold whipped mashed potatoes, two or three green fresh fall vegetables from the local farm and the finishing flair was an open house evening of a smorgasbord of desert wines, cognac, and Joyce's pies, cheese cake, flourless chocolate cake, baklava, chocolate rum balls and so much more. My holiday table was consistently beautiful, graced with the magnificent tablecloth that I had bought years ago in Nice, hand blown crystal, and always a new and interesting centerpiece. Great thought, care and planning went into this annual grand production.

Over the years I have accumulated a trove of cookware, dishes, china serving paraphernalia of every sort. In the past three years I have hosted dinner a handful times for friends, but for the most part, my beautiful dishes and company ware remain unused, gathering dust, superfluous, along with the memories of what had been a terribly meaningful part of my life.

Sad.

No One To Nurture

I was born in 1945, the year that World War II ended. Didn't really know the Great Depression or even that war; my parents had. But, indeed, that natal year was special for me. In fact, as I look back there had been a four to five year window of birth years between 1943 and 1947 that gave rise to an interesting phenomenon in *women* born then.

✣

Two banks held the supports for this unlikely coupling. The forties had spawned us and the fifties had suckled us on the teat of the eternal domestic: the nurturer, the soother of men, the smoother of the nest, the mother eternal. But the sixties had exploded into our teenage psyches. We answered the call of The Rolling Stones, we dared to challenge the world with our power, we were on the Pill and we loved sex and not the sex our mothers had endured. The world, the home, the demure, the strumpet, the cook the professional, the mother, the wife, the lawyer, the teacher, the businesswoman... We were the superwomen caught forever in our endless struggle to hold onto both shores to somehow not drown. And we are still here—I am still here. I know

now that we were and are a paradox. We were the bridge; we were the in-betweeners.

�֍

So, add that little contradiction to the austere truth of the aloneness.

✖

Better I had been born into one of the later generations of the hedonism of the sixties and seventies or the narcissism of the eighties, so I could drown in the dark pool of self-pity or puff up in the haze of self-importance.

❖

Better I had no desperate need to serve, to nurture, to love.

Those surviving spouses who are lucky enough to have an extended family as a support net, children and grandchildren near by, may fare better than I in dealing with the aloneness. Since my children live across the country and I have no grandchildren, I can only conjure up fantasies of closeness that this familial network would offer.

Zoning Out—The Fall

Of course, after Mel died, I went online to search out all the stages of grief, all the symptoms, all the dangers. I learned from the net that "zoning" can be dangerous. So, I was vigilant. I would talk to myself before I got behind the wheel of my truck: "Focus, Stay in the moment, Concentrate." Living in a three-story Victorian house with lethal staircases meant

more mantras! "Hold onto the railing. Slow
down. Be careful."

❖

*Each time I pulled out a sharp knife to mince
an onion I continued the drill of this endless
awareness to guard against slipping into that
vague zone of not being present, of drifting
into a nowhere place and so putting myself in
mortal danger and possibly chopping off my
fingers.*

❖

*So, who the hell would think a leisurely af-
ter-dinner seven o'clock evening summer walk
around the block could spell catastrophe?*

❖

Just finished eating. Had barbequed a piece of meat to eat with my salad. Was sitting on my front wrap-around porch as I am wont to do after dinner in the summer. Was lazy and guilty—earlier had been gardening in my rubber Croc shoes, yet pangs of guilt prevailed as I had for months stopped going to the gym. These recriminations urged me to *walk* my lazy ass around the block.

I should have changed into sneakers. Half way around the block and I had just passed my friend Jeannie's house. Somehow the toe of the rubber croc caught on the uneven blacktop.

❖

I plunged pell-mell face to meet the pavement. My glasses and upper arms helped to cushion the fall, but I had ripped the flesh between my left nostril and upper lip and broken my nose. Blood was everywhere soaking my bright yellow shirt and my white three-quarter cargo pants; the flood turned the ecru Crocs into a medley of scarlet. Yet, somehow, I found my way to Jeannie's door. I was traumatized, abstracted into a state of barely conscious numbness.

❖

Then came the hospital and the Cat scan mercifully saying I had no concussion but did have a minor fracture in my nose, not visible like the swollen nasty laceration just above my lip. Later, I went to a plastic surgeon because as the rip healed, my upper lip was being pulled upward to my nostril granting me the look of some kind of surreal Porky Pig. Charming image indeed. Luckily this doctor gave me the best and least invasive advice possible: get vitamin E oil and pull down on the lip a hundred times a day. And I did it, so that in six months the lip was normal, and now I am left with a scar only I notice when I have my glasses on. This could have ended badly. Damn, was I lucky!

Is there a smug truth to this bloody episode? I wish there were. I wish I could tell you that there is some logical, cognitive plan to avoid dropping into this somnam-bulistic state.

❖

All I can say is to be aware, to know that this type of accident can and indeed may happen to you. The best you can do is minimize the risks-the palpable dangers in your life and hope you have won the game of statistical advantage until you pass through this stage of grieving.

❖

Learning to Live With Spousal Loss

As we all get older unless we have had an enchanted existence, we must learn to live with disappointment and loss. Our children have grown up, have left or fled the natal nest and are pursuing their own lives. Our spouses and we have aged. We expect things to change and we adapt to, rail against or deny what we cannot change. But *this* is *different*.

❦

When we get married, nobody really thinks about the "till death do we part" part of the marriage vow. Romantic, idealistic, two well preserved gray haired octogenarians with beatific nitwit smiles walking hand-in-hand in an impressionistic flower-splashed meadow fading into the horizon...that is the fantasy that nobody really believes. Or do they? Who the hell wants to envision the end hooked up to intravenous tubes and Folely catheters?

❦

So, what is the reality? If you're married and if you stay married, one partner will ultimately predecease the other. And if we throw some statistics about projected longevity into the soup, more surviving partners will be women.

What comes to mind is a line by Willy Loman's wife in Arthur Miller's *Death of a Salesman.* It goes something like this, "Life is a casting off." And this line is somewhat sad, but comforting because we relinquish the outdated pieces of our lives little by little. I remember the little pangs with each ending— my children growing up, their leaving, retiring from teaching high school, and just three years ago shutting down my SAT business.

But death is total. Life simply ends. Sometimes death comes unexpected; more often today it is the culmination of a protracted illness. What does that mean for *you*, the one who is left?

✤

Now your life partner is gone. So, you now must begin a process of disengaging yourself from the fibrous connections that hold long-term marriages together. What is grieving, actually? As time passes, what you are actually doing is day-by-day emotional surgery.

✤

The Grand Delusion: The Superwoman Complex

I remember thinking how lucky I was to have the survival skills that I needed to go it alone. I had worked outside of the home full time during most of my married life. Had taught high school English for the better part of thirty years. Had started, taught and administered a successful SAT preparation business for 29 years. Had shopped, cooked, chauffeured, managed the finances. Had cleaned the house, weeded the flower beds, trimmed the shrubs and a host of so many other things in the myriad of tasks tacked onto the job of being wife and mother. I knew how to juggle all these demands and responsibilities and how to perform admirably and perfectly in each and every one of them. Good for me!

❖

So I knew how to pay the bills. So I knew how to make the phone calls to enlist the aid of those needed to maintain the house. So I knew how to call the lawyer and the accountant to take care of business.

So I was not a disenfranchised Stepford wife or arm candy now caught in limbless no support. Clearly Joyce was Superwoman!

❖

You can see, I subscribed to the grand delusion of thinking that my multitasking strengths would be *enough* to carry me through this great trial. They were not.

Early on friends had encouraged me to join a bereavement support group or go see a grief counselor. In retrospect, I think either or both of these suggestions could have helped, but I don't *play well* with others and didn't want to join what I viewed as a grieving party. I just didn't want to. I believed that since I was totally functional and since I wasn't melted *silly putty* sloshing around on the floor, then I didn't need professional counseling and support. Instead, I reached out to friends and talked to them almost daily to work out my feelings. Also, my daughter called (and still does call) me every day during this entire time. After eighteen months of grieving, I felt that I had "healed" considerably. Well, I now know that there was much pain that I had not faced and not worked through.

In the *Fantasy and the Peril* you will learn that I was in a dating relationship that ended at the beginning of last summer. My emotional reaction to this ending was completely out of proportion to the length and weight of the interaction. Although I was completely functional in my daily life, inside I was melted. My doctor called it a post-traumatic stress reaction—this new loss was just a catalyst, a door opener that unleashed a tsunami of yet unresolved pain and suffering. I was emotionally swamped, gasping for air and clarity because I actually had not finished the grieving process. I am grateful that I am so much better now; the flood has receded, but there is an occasional backwash.

Loss and Your Identity

"**W**ho am I?" becomes the un-spoken question in the later aftermath of loss. Death of a spouse especially a long-term spouse spells two things: the termination of your life as it was and a reevaluation of that thing called who you are. So, then what defines you? How others perceive you? What you

were? Your daily activities and interactions?
How you perceive yourself?

If you are introspective and aware, then
loom these questions. Each time you eat dinner alone, the first Thanksgiving when you
are a guest, going to a wedding and sitting
at the non-couples odd ball table, you are
reminded of the fact that you are now per-
ceived very differently by those around you.
On the first Thanksgiving after Mel's death
I ate at my girlfriend's house. But the second year was a disaster. I chose not to travel
to either of my children because flying on
holiday weekends is a nightmare. For more
than forty years I had hosted Thanksgiving,
lavishly. So, many people had sat at my table. This time no one thought to ask *me* what
I was doing for this national festivity. And
what happened was I sat home alone for the
first time and ate a tuna fish sandwich.

❖

I felt deserted, betrayed, diminished. Yet, the cognitive part of my brain told me that friends have their own families and their own obligations and their own lives and nobody owes me anything.

❖

Still, it hurt. Deeply. What is interesting is that all of this pain came not just from a feeling of abandonment or betrayal. I was in pain because I was yearning for what had been comfortable, for what had given me joy and validation. I had not made the jump from *We* to *I*. The *Joyce* of the *We* had always been the hostess, the one who invited everyone else! I was mourning the great gap in my life that now opens each time another holiday approaches.

What has become poignantly clear to me now in the three years since Mel's death is that the old life is also dead. What I now realize is that for a good part of that time I had been holding onto the old paradigm, the old life model thinking of how to replace some of what I had lost. I thought I had moved on, but I really hadn't. I am no longer part of a couple. And even if I were, it would have to be a new couple, a different interaction.

❖

Hiding in the shadow of the old life and so nursing an illusion that you can go on as you were is terribly crippling and ultimately destructive. But, logically acknowledging this truth is not enough: you have to feel it in your gut. You have to grasp it viscerally. And then you have to proactively deconstruct the intricate workings of the old in order to build the new.

❖

The Hoard and The Catharsis

When our son Jon was in fifth grade, Mel started taking classes in karate. His interest in the martial arts grew exponentially over the next thirty something years, so that at the time of his death he possessed three black belts and had gained expertise in Japanese swordsmanship both Iaido and Kendo, ceremonial

and fighting. In addition to attending classes to achieve this end, he took weekly private
lessons with a master sword teacher.

In college, Mel had majored in eco-
nomics, so his aesthetic sense was not realized in the first part of our marriage as he
was immersed in the pragmatic routine of
making a living. When I first met Mel, he
would spend time playing Flamenco guitar
music on his classical guitar. This hobby also
was shelved for years during the time of ek-
ing out a living. I, on the other hand, had
always indulged my sense of the arts as I had
majored in English in both my undergradu-
ate and graduate studies, so my love of liter-
ature (especially poetry) was just part of who
I was, and since I was teaching high school
English, I could indulge my passion for great
writers while I performed my job.

Growing out of Mel's interest in the martial arts came a fascination with Japanese antiques, at first musho ningyo—Japanese warrior dolls that were given to Japanese boy children on a holiday called Boy's Day. Mel's affiliation with a business customer had grown into a friendship and a professional relationship as the latter was a dealer in these Japanese dolls.

So, over time, Mel accumulated a sizable number of these figures. Each night he would sit behind his computer monitor and learn more and more about this collection, and then he branched out to collect and to research Japanese cloisonné, ceramics, ivory, and so much more. He was amassing quite a sophisticated collection and over time an amazing and intricate knowledge of several genres of Asian art. His research and his

knowledge were precise, subtle and huge. I
was truly in awe of all he knew.

During this time I did not object to his
accumulation as most of this inventory was
not only valuable, it was beautiful. Slowly
it adorned every room in the house; even
the walls held antique Japanese wood block
prints. Then, about three years before he
fell ill, he went *nuts.* It started when he had a
web site built to house his "retirement" business, called Mel's Antiques.

I think a wire in his brain disconnected
as he began buying and hoarding all kinds of
"antiques" and collectibles—most of them of
low quality and value. I live in a three- story
real Victorian home. So, he stuffed this crap
in the front-to-back dormers on the third
floor. His third floor office was packed ceil-
ing to floor. Four rooms in the basement left

no room to breathe. And the last space to be bulged was the oversized shed in the back yard. Thank God I don't have a garage!

�֍

Just before he was diagnosed with cancer, I had a major shit fit and threatened to start trashing all of the stuff if he did not de-clutter my home and rent a storage unit. As I am not a screamer and because I am a crazy clean neat freak, this histrionic display was effective: he believed me. As fate would have it, the cleansing never happened as illness crashed in the door and the hoard was no longer significant.

✖

Irony of ironies! Mel was dead and now all the *stuff* from the sublime and beautiful to the ridiculous and hackneyed was mine. Now, it was all *my stuff.* And I had absolutely no desire to run his antique business. Two weeks before he died, I sat for three hours and printed out all the pages of his Mel's Antiques website. I needed to keep the tome of pages that held the photos, descriptions and prices of the best of Mel's collections. Then, I shut the site down. A very powerful moment.

A week after he died when things had begun to quiet down, I actually took a *look* at the volume of inventory, some treasure, some junk, that I was facing. I sat on the floor outside Mel's office, mesmerized. Where to begin?

I enlisted help. First, I hired the handy-man and his helper and directed them to completely clear out the third floor dormers. Collectibles went to the basement, bags went to good will, and piles of junk went to the street. If I could have just chucked all of this great stash, the solution would have been simple. Then I would have rented a large dumpster and have emptied all into the waiting receptacle. But mixed insanely among the junk were museum quality treasures. So, I had to meticulously check everything as the men worked.

Next, I called Mel's friend who is an antiques middleman and did so at Mel's behest. He was invaluable in helping me vet and sell some of the inventory. This process went on for eighteen months and then culminated in a three-day huge tag sale. After the sale, I donated anything that did not sell to the Viet Nam Vets. I had vowed that nothing would come back into my house.

Through that first summer, fall, and then winter, I remember stuffing in huge plastic bags 350 (yes, I said 350!) Norman Rockwell collector plates still housed in their cardboard shipping containers. I couldn't sell them because they had no resale value— it seems as I was told that they were a false collectible. I would drag these heavy Santa sacks of garbage up the cellar stairs, across the lawn and out to the street—cursing Mel the entire time for leaving me with this awful mess. I knew the answer was to start in one corner and keep on plugging day after day.

The shed was another nightmare. Stowed on the overhead shelf and anywhere else in this storage unit were over one hundred, hundred-year old wooden boxes that originally held the Japanese dolls. They were fragile and filthy. Dressed in goggles and armed with leather gloves and a huge hammer, I sat on a blue plastic tarp on my driveway and smashed those buggers. Can

you visualize this? Then, I bagged the debris
and out to the street it went.

❖

*It took a daily effort for a year and a half to
cleanse my home. I originally felt my anger
stemmed only from having to clean up someone
else's mess—a job I had never volunteered
for. Later, I came to know that my rage
at all of this unfinished business was really
my outrage at Mel for having the audacity to
leave me!*

❖

I continued pushing through with the
cleaning out process. One day I made 57 trips
up and down two flights of stairs and then
outside to the handy man's pickup truck.
Thirteen years of *Art and Antiques* magazines

(they're big, glossy and heavy) and an entire bookcase full of fat hardbound antiques reference guides now made obsolete by the information availability on the internet were chucked into the flatbed of the pickup truck ready for the dump!

In the autumn of 2011 came one of the last steps in the purging, the huge tag sale. Having it orchestrated by a professional to sell the middling level collectibles was essential. Inventory filled at least 20 tables lining the wrap around first level porch and most of the front yard. Profit was not my motive; everything was priced significantly below cost so that it would move. Much sold and what did not was donated. I had achieved my goal: not one piece from this sale came back into my house.

The volume of inventory of collectibles was daunting, so I am thankful I did not personally conduct the sale. Consequently, I did not deal with any of the customers or the transactions. Although it was amazingly therapeutic for me to get all this *stuff* gone, the physical act of seeing Mel's possessions, things he had saved and treasured, things that now were just *things* departing was painful for me. I couldn't help being profoundly moved.

❖

It was an eerie feeling indeed watching strangers cart off all the "pieces" of Mel. What I am saying is that this whole process really was in truth a palpable disassembly of the old life.

❖

You Can Do It!

❖

About a year before Mel got sick, I spent more than three thousand dollars on a generator and then had my trusty electrician install it with a professional circuit board! Mel told all our friends that my motivation had been to protect and preserve my stash of homemade frozen pies that I had lined up in my freezer in the basement. The way he figured it,

I had invested between five and six hundred dollars per pie.

❖

I have been making pies every year since I was a small child. Each year I would have strawberry/rhubarb, peach and apple pies shelved in my freezer ready to be baked and enjoyed. I hate to admit it, but there was some truth in Mel's assessment. I also insisted that we order a sturdy plastic shed to house the machine and purchased four five-gallon plastic red gasoline containers. In any case, we never needed nor used the generator in his lifetime.

But, in the early fall of 2011, Hurricane Irene came barreling across Long Island and left me without power for five days! Had Mel been alive, the job of turning on, filling with fuel, tending to the generator would not have been a thought of mine. He was the man, and he would have taken care of all of it. In the past, the only machinery I operated was my automobile or my kitchen appliances. I am lucky that my electrician lives across the street and is also my friend; he taught me how to operate the 6500 watt generator. But the hourly and daily chore of pouring gasoline, operating the zones all fell to me. I simply had to learn or else I could sit like a helpless fool in the dark.

❧

Lo and behold as I sit here this day and write this entry, I am reliving last year but with a greater punch. Hurricane Sandy is pressing down hard now with 70-80 mph gusts—power is out and probably will be for several days.

❖

On Saturday I had my handyman fill the four large gasoline containers, put all porch furniture etc, safely away in the shed. I had earlier in the week stocked up on D batteries, bottled water. Right now the generator is humming—running the refrigerator, the freezer, the kitchen lights.

❖

Before I go to bed I have to brave the winds, the dark, my fears and shut down the machine for the night—carrying my battery operated lantern through the wind and driving rain then return to a dark house and go to bed only to venture out again in the morning in the rain and refill the tank and restart my red power machine.

❖

I'm writing this on my laptop with 67% battery remaining. My iPhone isn't working because it's blowing like hell out there and the signals are not going through. Thank heaven for the generator or I'd be very much alone in the dark.

Ok, it's tomorrow. St. James looks like a war zone. Trees are down everywhere, many crushing houses. Have no access to television, so I have very incomplete knowledge. I've heard that NYC, Staten Island and New Jersey were devastated. I lost two big trees, but there was no damage to my house. 90% of Long Island is presently without power. I run my generator six hours in the morning and six hours in the evening. I turn the machine off during most of the day and all night to conserve fuel. It's not as scary tonight because the storm has passed. Was outside visiting with neighbors—walked around the neighborhood to survey the damage. It was warm today in the mid-sixties, but I know the weather is about to turn colder. Made coffee for some neighbors who have no power. There has been a real sense of community here.

Went to bed after I ventured out into the dark again last night at eleven o'clock to turn off the generator. Now, it's almost 6:30 a.m. and I'm sitting here with two Coleman battery powered lanterns writing this until the sun rises. I have to fill the generator with gasoline before I turn it on...getting cold— the temperature dropped last night so I'll have to turn on heat today. Am wearing yesterday's dirty clothes until I can power up, wait for hot water, then shower. Hey, at least I have these options.

❖

Well, I thought I'd write a continuation as I am still living a continuation of this insane "camping" adventure. The power went out eight days ago, and my town has the "distinction" of being one of three on Long Island to be restored last!

❖

I have been mostly "tied " to the house, ventured out only twice to get a paper because I can't risk using up my gasoline. Gas lines have been two miles long—violent tempers at the pump even with police presence have become commonplace. My last resort if I run out of gasoline for the generator is to siphon it out of my truck! I awoke this morning (after waking about every two hours all night) to temps in the thirties. My house had stayed at about sixty or so because I had cranked up the heat on the third floor that houses my bedroom before I turned off the generator for the night.

Trekked out to the shed at 5:45 a.m. to unlock the coveted gasoline, poured the golden liquid out of the five-gallon jugs into my plastic pitcher into the waiting generator, pulled out the choke, turned on the ignition, and Viola! I keep telling myself not to stress out because at least my home has no damage, I have managed to get gas for the generator and so on.

❖

Have you ever tried to talk yourself out of a low level stress that is no longer low level? Good luck, Joyce.

❖

Last night got together with two neighbor families (my kids' ages) and pooled our food. Their kids call me Grandma Mrs. Benson and I love it. Lisa came here with two of her brood of five to cook the Italian sausage with broccoli rabe replete with pasta on my professional gas stove while I heated up my leftover brisket and potatoes and boiled more pasta for my defrosting pesto. Threw together a big salad. I had gone to the farm stand around the corner earlier and grabbed the rest of some still good produce. It reminded me of my youth in Rochester when this kind of "community" sharing was the norm. I guess I have lived in an upper-middle class suburb so long that I'd almost forgotten the richness of that human fabric.

I sit here now in yesterday's clothes, unshowered, downing mugs of black coffee, waiting for the water to heat up, so I can shower and join the human race!

❖

Is there a moral to this engaging tale? Of course.

The universe doesn't give a hoot if a hurricane is roaring, if your power is out, if a blizzard buries you in feet of snow. Realize it. Know it that you are alone and you must empower yourself.

❖

The Fantasy and the Peril

In August of 2011, my friends convinced me to join two online dating services. Shortly thereafter I had two "dates." The first was simply coffee at Starbucks with a man who had been divorced for over 25 years. When I asked him what he was looking for in a woman, he responded, "Sweet." Well, I looked straight at him and told him that in 66 years many adjectives had been used to describe me, and *sweet* wasn't on the list! When he told me his younger son was a paranoid schizophrenic who was dangerous, I looked at my watch and excused myself. End of that meeting.

The next encounter was less creepy but just as terminal. This gentleman who was my age was from a rural area in Massachusetts, took the jet boat across the Sound and met me at the tip of the north fork of Long Island. We spent a beautiful summer day, had lunch, walked, talked—nice man. He stayed four hours longer than he had planned, but I think we both knew that had we met 40 years ago…maybe. As we ate lunch, he looked at my purple nail and toenail polish and asked if everybody on Long Island had purple nails. He was lovely and so was the day. We were both just from different planets.

For the next couple of weeks the only men who responded to me online were ten to fifteen years older than I. Just what I needed at age 66—an octogenarian on oxygen! The ugly truth is that men still have the advantage. If they are healthy, fit and have money they can and do get much younger women. Something's never seem to change: women will prostitute themselves to a codger if he's well-heeled. I guess that statement is a depressing commentary on both sexes. So, I took my name off both sites and never went back to that virtual meat rack.

In the fall of 2011 Mel had been dead a good eighteen months. I was feeling centered and stable and had not needed any Xanax support for several months. What I didn't know was that I was prime meat, sittin' duck, ripe for the pickins,' whatever the hell cliché you want to dub the real vulnerability and gullibility that would spew pain onto my life for months to come. When I started writing this book, I meant to leave this commentary out. But now, I feel that omitting this story would leave others open to the emotional jeopardy that caused me to ignore my instincts, ignore my brain and be swept away by my need, my desire to be desired.

I didn't meet him in a bar. I didn't find him online. I knew him. Had known him for more than two years. He was attractive, intelligent, cosmopolitan. He pursued me, diligently. And I was swept away by the wave, dated him from that fall until the beginning of summer. I was not blind nor deaf; I saw and heard all of the signs and warnings. I knew his history—women for him had been temporary couplings, that's all. I was simply the current relationship. So, I went with it: saw the fantasy man and looked away from the real man who had never promised me anything, never lied to me, and all to my peril and certainly not to his. I gave my heart; it's what I do, what women do when we care for someone. I should have guarded it better

So, at this writing I am again alone, have been for several months. My purpose here is not to crucify him nor to rail against myself. Rather, it is to warn others that after the death of a long-term spouse, after the dismantling of a life, after profound loss there is profound need and profound vulnerability. Be very careful. If you can. Had it not been this man, it probably would have been another. That is the uncomfortable truth I see. The dating market out there even at my age is not filled with Prince Charmings waiting to carry you away on their white steeds. It can be a vast wasteland filled with great peril to you unless you keep your vision honest and clear.

Now, I am moving forward again in the rhythm of my life, a little smarter than I was before. Another thought. Should I have avoided this relationship? Should I have hidden myself away in the third floor dormer and not taken the chance on this part of life? How about you, what should you do? I guess the answer is personal and individual. For me, there is only the reality of who I am and have always been. I have and do dare and risk and push forward the frontiers of my life; now, I just hope to do it better.

Knitting It Together

Sometimes a mug of good rich black coffee is quite a clarifier.

❖

I remember shortly after Mel's death a couple of people actually had the audacity to ask me if I were angry, angry at God, angry at the universe, that he had died.

❖

After all, he had done everything right, ate low fat, low sodium natural foods, worked out every day, didn't smoke, drank little and to top it off he was, as everybody who knew him said, a *good guy*. Interesting question. It leads to more. Why him? Why now? Does it gnaw at me? Do I seek the answer? No and no.

How did Mel embrace his death? Simply. He just wouldn't acknowledge it. He granted only life entrance into his consciousness, his mind, his spirit. That's why he wouldn't answer my questions about his final arrangements.

❖

Death just wasn't in his vocabulary, ever. Over the 22 months of his illness he lived each minute of his life—he lived his dying and he lived it well.

❖

The last week Mel stopped talking. He was awake and he was aware. He no longer needed words. This was a powerful silence— for me who is and has always been the word-smith. Words just ceased; they weren't need-ed. The last couple of days when I was with him all he wanted was for me to kiss him. He wanted me with him then. He wanted me to see him out, the consummate expression of love. I had never been closer to him, to anyone.

❖

He graced me with these last moments of his life and his death. They were ethereal—what I felt is almost ineffable—hard to craft into words. His end of journey to his passing gave me an amazing spiritual gift. He was here in this realm in the world of life and simultaneously he was touching the other, and I was touched by both.

❖

So, you might ask if I became a *believer*. Well, I grew up in a rather strict Jewish home; early on I had rejected the ritual and abandoned being an observant Jew. Over the decades, I kept the cultural parts of my Jewish heritage that I love. I didn't have to *find* a belief because I have always *had* my spiritual comfort in a greater power. Then, how did these last moments of Mel's life, powerful and transcendent, impact me? I didn't become a *believer*. No. I became a *knower*. I came to *know* the soft beauty of dying. I came to *know* the peace. Mel has granted me a grand gift—I no longer fear death.

Another question: "Would I like to talk to Mel now if I could?" My answer again is no. There would be nothing to say. There was no unfinished business between us.

❖

It had been complete and completion needs nothing more.

❖

An Uneven Number

It was a Friday evening last fall; I had invited two couples whom I care a great deal about to an elegant dinner here at my home. Earlier in the week I had dragged two leaves of the dining table down two flights of stairs from their storage place in the third floor dormer. With much difficulty I pulled open the table and managed to inset the leaves, push the table halves back together to do a two-man job alone. Ironed the company table linens, washed the beautiful raised gold cobalt blue Aynsley china, polished the silver and lined all this beautiful dinnerware on the dining room sideboard, then covered it to keep it dust free. Thursday night I raided my big basement freezer and baked off an apple pie and a strawberry rhubarb.

The first wave of shopping I had done earlier in the week, but the perishables, the must-be-fresh items had to wait until Friday morning. I made five stops—fresh asparagus from Whole Foods, chicken breasts from my butcher, salad greens from Trader Joe's, the good Italian bread from my local pasta store—the rest from the local supermarket. And then I began cooking. Worked all day, finished the preparations about four o'clock, then cleaned up the kitchen before I showered, shampooed and primped for the evening. This was all quite tiring as I'm not 25 anymore and the amount of work would have been daunting even for a youngster.

But that's not my point.

The best part of preparing a dinner party is setting the table. I have always reserved this job for myself—I guess it's an adult excursion into playing tea party! Setting the table *this* time was bittersweet. I set it for five. Two couples. And then me.

❖

The uneven number was the testament to where I am now, to what I am feeling, to what I miss, to what I need, to what I want. I am an uneven number.

❖

Move On

Today is Saturday in early January 2013 and it truly is an amazing day. Today, I traded words for action. Two nights ago, Thursday evening, I was in great pain. Not the angst of grief from the death of Mel, not the emptiness of losing that other man who is now a phantom, no, something more acute, like the cut of a razor sharp blade.

All of my words about moving on seemed static, stuck, actionless, without punch. I was frozen, motionless here in the shadow of the old life. I *really* hadn't moved on.

❖

The poignant pain was the pain of slavery, of entrapment. And I was both the slave and the slave master, both the trapped and the trap.

❖

When I woke up Friday morning (yesterday) and cleared the morning haze out of my psyche with the usual three mugs full of black coffee, I knew that last night's pain had *sliced* through to the truth. I could never be free while I stayed in this house. So, I called the real estate agent who is also my friend.

We spoke, we made a verbal contract and he came here today and I signed the written contract—the house would be on market in three days. I have been working relentlessly packing away the visible clutter to stage the house for showing—done this before so I know the drill. By Tuesday, the house was photo-ready, the listing was posted on MLS, the sign was erected on the front lawn and action had replaced words.

❖

I am not my house. I am not my car. I am not my town and all the familiar haunts and people therein. These are all the trappings of my comfort zone. I am not things nor places nor other people.

❖

I face these as my truths. I accept these so that I can leave my house, leave my town, leave all that has been familiar for 42 years and drive across country and begin life anew in the desert in the foothills of the mountains of Arizona. My house has been put up for sale again, I will sell it, I will go. And I will not "go meekly" into my new life.

The Second Life

Searching for and finding the end for my narrative has been an introspective and revealing process. Was chatting with Joel on the phone this morning and he just hit a simple phrase that points to the direction of this journey, where my life must go now. *A second life!*

What has actually happened to me in the past three plus years? First, the initial re-actions to Mel's death and to the death of the first life: the shock, the pain, the anxiety, the cleaning out and the organizing of first my physical environment and then my psy-che, the mistakes, the misconceptions. Then came the struggle: the coming to terms with the dismantling and the discarding of the first life. And now, I am at times a little wob-bly, but mostly I am energized, excited to be facing the new.

❧

The old life is gone. The old doesn't work. Death of my spouse has ended the old. I didn't choose it. It isn't fair. It is painful. It is terrifying. And, yet, it is liberating. OK, then what is the second life? How does it start? When? Where does it go? This

is a beginning, a birth—it is vast potential!
And birth is bare and birth is new.

❖

Here's what I know, absolutely. It's not about your kids or your friends or whatever the *How To* books preach. It's all about you. You make the second life. You refashion yourself. This is all very uncertain and it is all very simple.

Start with the known. Build from firm ground. Ask pivotal questions. In fact, write them down and then answer them: What is important to me? What gives meaning to my life?

And so, I have been taking stock in Who I am.

I am a woman. I am pretty, feminine and sexy. I am a completer of a man. After the death, that woman died. Last year *she* was resurrected—*she* rediscovered her grove, she lost 25 pounds, *she* went to the gym and toned up, *she* bought seductive clothing, *she* learned *she* could and did love another man and all at the age of 66. And even though that other man is gone from her life, that woman in her, in me is alive and vibrant.

I am a friend. Those that I leave behind in the East, those who are my true friends will remain so. There is the telephone, there is email, there is the airplane. Leaving St. James does not spell the end to those meaningful people whom I love and who love me. Certainly, I have precedent for this fact: Jackie and I have been friends now for 51 years and the time and the distance (she lives in upstate NY) have not compromised the depth or truth of that bond.

❖

Grieving has been an inward trial. It is poking around in the dark places of your soul, your mind, your emotions. It's a sticky trap if you stay too long languishing in your pain, grasping at the ghosts of your loss.

❖

So. The new journey is not an inward probing, it is not metaphysical—rather it is facing outward—moving going and doing and creating. It is the spirit of youth—the spirit of life. And I am grateful that I am well equipped to step out into life to create the new, the second life. I am a worker, I am a doer, I am a creator.

I am a soul that yearns to love and to nurture and be loved and be nurtured. I know that I will form new connections and new relationships and move forward as I reach out to others in my second life. Going through the anguish and the pain that all started in May 2008 when Mel was diagnosed with cancer and continuing into last summer, the summer of the pts tsunami, has taught me great humility. It has softened me, but not weakened me. I am proud to say that I know how to love, deeply, to give of my heart totally. Yes, I have taken and do take the risks that come with this openness of the heart. But I will live my life no other way!

I am a thinker and a seeker. Perhaps that is why I switched my major from math and science to English so many decades ago. That is why I have loved to read and study the literary masters, most of the past. That is why

I have probed philosophy, Zen, metaphysics, religions. And I don't think that part of me will take up too much space in my truck as I roll westward.

I am a teacher, a master teacher, and I love teaching. I always knew I would be a teacher. As a young child, I would arrange my stuffed animals in a semi-circle and teach imaginary lessons. Continued my mock classroom all through junior high and high school without the stuffed animals as I paced around my room gesticulating as I *studied* aloud my notes from history and chemistry. (I didn't play with girly dolls, hated them, still do. In fact, when I was ten, I put my Barbie doll under the wheels of a bus and watched it get crunched—good grief you *shrinks* out there can have a field day with that snippet!)

I remember my first reaction eons ago when I first performed in a classroom, "I'm getting *paid* to do this?" And forty-eight years later, I feel the same way. I have never stopped loving the kids nor loving the art of teaching. I feel blessed that so long ago I answered my "calling' and I know that I don't have to and shouldn't give up this so very significant part of my being. My husband knew it too. Two days before he died he gave me three short injunctions. One was, "Don't give up the tutoring. You need it." And he didn't mean money.

❖

So now, at the starting gate of my second life I look to a different classroom, a different venue to continue to learn and to teach like the cleric in Chaucer's "Canterbury Tales," "gladly lerne and gladly teche." And this book is my first step into that new classroom and in it I am joyful.

❖

www.ingramcontent.com/pod-product-compliance
Lightning Source LLC
Chambersburg PA
CBHW060257050426
42448CB00009B/1667